Praise for "*Doggy Celebrates Christmas*"

What a wonderful book to share with young children or grandchildren during the Christmas holidays! "Ella", the dog, is showcased in a variety of Christmas and holiday settings--from decorating the tree, to the nativity, and even Christmas cookies! I am particularly impressed with how the author is able to write a book with simple to understand sentences, then lead the child/children into using higher level thinking skills through carefully orchestrated questions concerning the picture or event. As a dog lover, I love this little book about a much-loved family's pet, and I fully intend to read it to my youngest grandchildren. I also think this book would be a great reading resource for primary school teachers (lower grades), as well as parents and grandparents.

Marialex, grandmother

Ella the Doggy is a must-have children's series. This latest story captures Ella as the holiday approaches. She observes the preparations and checks out the decor. Oh, my goodness, there's a cliff hanger: Will Ella get a cookie? I'll never tell. You'll have to read this charmer yourself. The images are picture perfect, the narrative draws your child into the story and questions invite your child to actively engage. An absolute win.

LEADistics, (review on Amazon)

This is such a great book to read with children, especially during the Holiday season when families gather together. It would be a wonderful gift to make some happy memories with. "Doggy's Busy Day" is easy to read and all the doggy pictures are so fun to look at. The book makes you want to snuggle up with your kids, grab some hot chocolate and then jump into the story. I can guarantee you that you will love this book!

Makiko David, mother of four

· ·

"*Doggy Celebrates Christmas*"
is dedicated to everyone who can still remember
celebrating Christmas as children do, with awe and excitement!

Jayne Flaagan

If you enjoyed "*Doggy Celebrates Christmas*," please leave a review with Amazon. This will help other families learn about Ella the doggy too! Click here to leave your review if you are on a Kindle.

If you are reading this book in paperback, you can copy and paste the following link in your browser to leave a review:

http://www.amazon.com/gp/product/B00PBII7I8

Also, don't forget to look for Ella's other books!

Thank you!

Ella (the doggy) and Jayne (the author)

Visit www.ellathedoggy.com now!

This is a picture of Ella the Doggy's first Christmas.

She is sitting with her best friend Camper.

Ella is the small puppy with the big ears!

This is how big Ella is today!

She is five and a half years old.

How old are you?

A few weeks before Christmas, Ella the doggy sees a big green tree in the living room.

She thinks the tree should be decorated.

Do you know what the word "*decorate*" means?

Ella watches while pretty lights are put on the tree.

Then the tree is decorated with ornaments.

What are your favorite Christmas decorations?

Did you see the beautiful angel on top of the tree?

In the living room Ell has found a small Santa.

Puppies and dogs sniff new things they find.

Is this Santa real?

Then Ella finds a tiny Christmas
tree wearing a Santa hat.

The Christmas tree has a face and it sings!

Isn't that silly?

Now Ella is wearing a Santa Claus hat.

Do you think she looks like Santa?

In the window, Ella sees a small Christmas village.

Village is another word for "*town.*"

What do you think Ella is looking at so closely?

Oh no! She knocked over the snowman with her nose!

It's okay.

Someone will stand the snowman back up again.

Here is Ella looking at the manger
where baby Jesus was born.

Do you know what a manger is?

Ella the doggy likes listening to Christmas stories.

Do you have a favorite Christmas story?

Ella sees lots of colorful lights outside too.

What kind of decorations are there?

Oh my! Pretty lights are everywhere!

Inside the house, someone has made
Christmas cookies and is eating them.

Do you think Ella will get a bite of a cookie?

Yes, Ella's friend shared a cookie with her!

What kind of cookie shapes are on the table?

Every Christmas Ella poses for a family picture.

Who is in your family?

The day before Christmas is called Christmas Eve.

On Christmas Eve, Ella's family has a special dinner.

What are your favorite foods?

Ella eats a special dinner too.

Look closely. Whose picture is on the bowl?

On Christmas morning, Ella looks for her gifts.

She has found her present and
is sniffing inside the bag.

What do you think her present is?

(You guessed right if you thought it was a bone).

Ella has found her stocking too.

What is that inside the stocking?

Yes, it is another bone!

Ella got two bones for Christmas!

This has made her very happy.

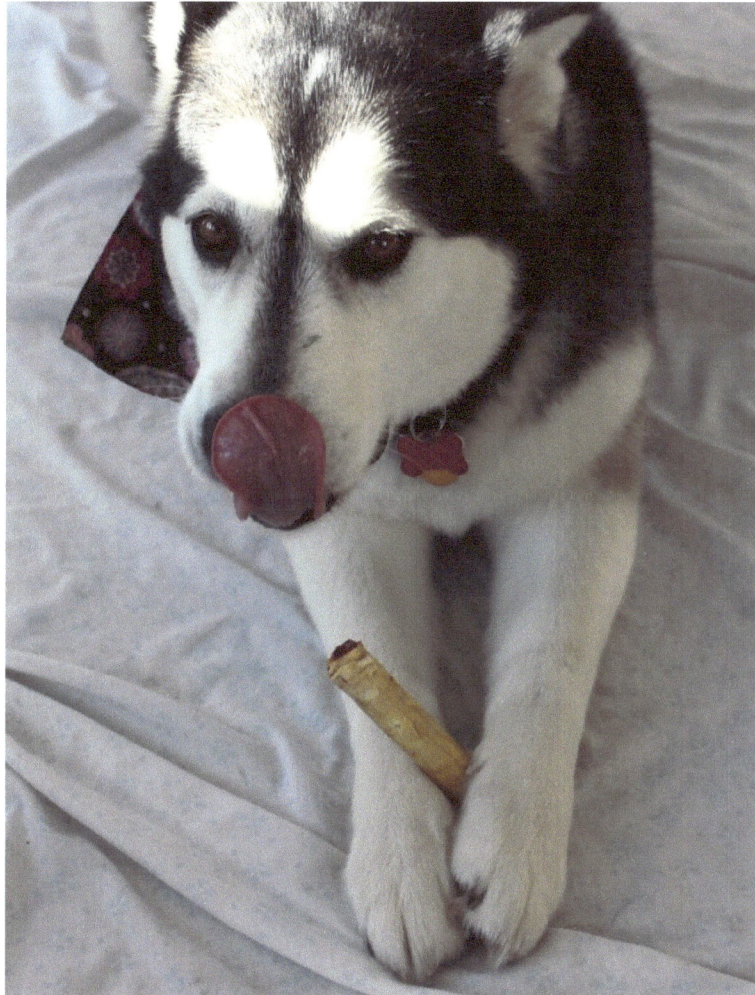

She wants you to have a happy Christmas too.

Merry Christmas and Happy New Year from
Ella the doggy!

Jayne Flaagan
Husky Publishing
East Grand Forks, MN
email: djflaagan@gra.midco.net

About the Author and Ella…

Jayne Flaagan grew up in North Dakota and made
the big move to Minnesota many years ago.
She lives with her husband and her goofy dog, Ella. She also has three adult children.

Flaagan has degrees in Advertising/Public Relations, Elementary Education and French. The author has a background of over 30 years in Elementary and Early Childhood education, as well an extensive expertise in writing for many different publications and in several different genres. She thoroughly enjoys writing for young readers.

The author speaks Spanish, loves to travel, read, do crossword puzzles, and spend time with her family, as well as having various other hobbies.
Books have always been a huge part of Flaagan's life and reading to children is something she feels is critical to every child's learning experience.
She estimates that she has probably read around a million books to children over the years!

Jayne Flaagan grew up on a farm with a Husky for a pet and she has many fond memories of him. When it was time to get a dog for her own family, she knew that it had to be a Husky. Huskies are fun, lovable and have lots of energy.
Ella has provided so much joy and entertainment for her own family that Flaagan decided she wanted to share Ella with other families. Thus, "***Ella the Doggy***" book series was born!

www.ellathedoggy.com

www.ingramcontent.com/pod-product-compliance
Lightning Source LLC
Chambersburg PA
CBHW041240040426
42445CB00004B/94